MW01133225

A GIRL'S GUIDE TO LIFE

by

Michelle Herman

with an introduction by Grace Herman-Holland
Illustrations by Glen Holland

Thought Catalog Books/Prospecta Press

Copyright © 2014 by Michelle Herman

Published by Thought Catalog Books a division
of The Thought & Expression Co., Williamsburg,
Brooklyn in association with Prospecta Press an
imprint of Easton Studio Press, LLC
P.O. Box 3131
Westport CT 06880
www.prospectapress.com

For general information address hello@
thoughtcatalog.com; for submissions to Thought
Catalog Books manuscripts@thoughtcatalog.
com. Founded in 2010, Thought Catalog is a
website and imprint dedicated to your ideas and
stories. We publish fiction and non-fiction from
emerging and established writers across all
genres. Learn more at www.thoughtcatalog.
com/about.

ISBN 978-1-63226-020-8

Printed in the United States of America
First Printing: December 2014

10 9 8 7 6 5 4 3 2 1

Cover illustration by Glen Holland

For Grace

and for her grandfather

Morton Herman
1930-2014

who, by his example, taught
the author of this book
nearly everything she knows
about how to live

INTRODUCTION

It's too bad that when we're born, there isn't somebody waiting to hand us a how-to guide and send us off to live easy, structured lives where we know all the rules and can't mess up. Of course there's no such thing—and there's a good reason for that: you are the only one with your mind and body, and nobody else is ever going to know just exactly what it is like to be you every day. You're lucky, because you're the only one who's ever going to be able to be you.

But sometimes being you isn't so easy. Some days you probably feel scared, or hurt, or nervous, or lonely, or sad, or angry. There may be times when you feel like you want somebody to tell you what you should do.

Maybe you don't ever feel that way. But when I was eight and a half that was how I felt. I had a best friend I loved very much, but she was a year and a half older and she felt differently about some things and we got into fights a lot. I was very nervous about getting older, making new friends, and having new teachers who I'd heard were strict and mean. At the time, my mother and I were reading *Little Women* together and I pointed out that for Christmas Meg, Jo, Beth, and Amy's mother gives each of them a "guide to life."

"That's what I want," I told my mother. "I want a guide to life, too."

I don't know if I wanted it because I was jealous that the sisters in the book got what I thought was such a cool Christmas present, or if I wanted it because of how scared and anxious I felt about growing up when I was eight and a half.

But either way, my mother wrote it for me.

Fast-forward ten years. The summer before I left home for the first time and went away to college many, many miles away, my then-boyfriend and I found a little white book, bound by hand with embroidery thread, on one of my bookshelves. It was the *Guide to Life.* I had forgotten all about it.

"I wonder what it says about love, and I wonder if it was right," I said, laughing. I sat him down and read the whole thing out loud to him.

It turned out that we both thought it *was* right—about love and about many other things, too. Even at eighteen, sometimes a girl needs someone—a mother, or someone else wise who she loves—to remind her that it's okay to say no, or that you should thank people when you're grateful, or that you should try to get to know people even when you're afraid they might not like you.

And now, three years later, as I'm getting ready to finish college and become a real adult who's supposed to be able to be wise and know what she wants and give her *own* advice, I've come back to the *Guide to Life.* Even though my fears now are a little bit different, because soon I'm going to start going to work instead of school, and the fights I have with my best friends are about different sorts of things, I still worry about growing up in the same way I did when I was eight and a half and I asked my mother for a "guide to life." Because here's the thing: Even as you get older, you're going to be the very same person you are now. And no matter how grown-up you become, it never hurts to be reminded of the things that are really important in life.

If you haven't already guessed it, this book *is* the *Guide to Life* that my mother wrote for me when I was a little girl worried about growing up. I hope it brings you some of the comfort and guidance it's brought me as I've come back to it and come back to it again as I've grown up. Nobody, not even your mother, or *my* mother, can tell you how to be you. But it's always nice to have someone to guide you.

– *Grace Herman-Holland*

PART ONE

The Right Thing

The truth is that no one, not even your parents, can tell you how to live your life.

Your parents, along with other adults—your grandparents, godparents, aunts and uncles, teachers, and others—can give you useful advice and tell you what helped them in their lives, but in the end everybody figures out "how to live" all by herself.

Still, there are some things—some basic kinds of things—that a wiser, older person can tell you that will help you as you begin to figure this out.

And that is what I propose to do.

Here is the first piece of advice:

Do the right thing.

Oh, sure, I know—it's easy for me to say, "Do the right thing," and it's easy for you to say, "Of course I will! Why would I ever want to do the *wrong* thing?"—but what *is* the right thing? How are you supposed to know?

Here's a thought worth keeping in mind about doing "the right thing": every philosophy and religion in the world includes some version of "the golden rule"—*Do unto others as you would have others do unto you*—as part of its teachings.

(Religion is a system of *belief*, a way of thinking about God, and there are lots and lots of different religions practiced by the human beings of the world. Philosophy is a system for *thinking* about things, and there are lots of different kinds of philosophies, or different ways of thinking about life, too.)

The world's religions and philosophies propose many different ways of believing and thinking, and as you get older you will have the chance to learn about them. But one thing they all have in common is the *golden rule*, which urges us to treat people the way we wish to be treated ourselves.

But how does this rule help you to do the right thing?

It has to do with something called *empathy*, which means imagining what it feels like to be someone else, or "putting yourself in her shoes." If you stop and think about how it would feel to *be* the other person, you can almost always figure out how to behave toward that person. (It's true that sometimes this is hard—and if the other person is very different from you, it may be *very* hard. But even when it's very hard, it is always worth attempting.)

People fail each other—they hurt each other—when they don't take into consideration what it would feel like to be that person.

The golden rule even helps when you're dealing with pets, not people—although it's possible to go overboard. (For example, when the author of this Guide was younger, she had cats, and she would sit perfectly still for hours if one of her cats happened to fall asleep on her lap. She would think, "Oh, how would I feel if *I* were happily asleep in a giant lap and I were forced to wake up and plopped right out of her lap?" So she couldn't move. She didn't want to be a mean giant.)

I don't think you can go overboard, though, when it comes to other human beings. The single best thing you can do, in dealing with people, especially when they're behaving badly, is to stop and ask yourself: How does it feel to be her (or him)? What might be causing her to act this way? If you do this—if you take the time to wonder what the other person is feeling—then instead of reacting quickly and being just as unpleasant as she is being, you will have given yourself a chance to think it through, and you are much more likely to do the right thing.

So—let's say—when a friend visits and is complaining and whining, saying, "It's not fair that you're calling this model horse [or Barbie, or American Girl doll, or set of markers] 'special' and saying I can't use it," maybe it would help if you imagined yourself *as* her for a moment, if you said to yourself, silently, *Okay, here I am, I'm in* her *house and we're playing a game and she won't let me use any of the things I most want to use.* And if you happen to have a lot of model horses/Barbies/American Girl dolls/sets of markers, and you know that she doesn't have many at her house—or if you have a lot more things of all kinds than she does—try asking yourself how it would feel to be her, being told that certain of your things are off limits. It may not be easy to pretend to be that other girl, but try it anyway. Ask yourself: *How does it feel to be her? What would I be saying if I felt the way she's feeling right now? What would I be doing?* And even if turns out that you wouldn't do or say any of the things your friend is doing or saying, trying this out in your mind may help you to figure out a way to handle the situation. You'll find that this feels much better than getting frustrated—which would probably lead to you losing your temper.

If you do lose your temper (and sometimes this is bound to happen—sometimes things will happen that will leave you so frustrated, confused, or angry that no amount of "thinking things through" or imagining what it feels like to be the other person can keep you from being just plain mad), it's a good idea to remind yourself, and to remind your friend too, that everyone gets angry sometimes, and that feeling angry isn't the end of the world. (You might even have to remind your friend that *she* gets angry sometimes too—which is a way to help *her* take a moment to imagine what it feels like to be *you*!)

Once you've gotten your frustration out of your system, though, remember to pause and think about how it feels to be yelled at—and that should help you to apologize (see below for some more thoughts on apologizing). It's important to know that no matter how much you like someone, you will probably get irritated and even furious at her once in a while—and she will probably feel the same way about you from time to time. Learning how to deal with being disappointed or angry is part of growing up, and learning how to express these feelings to the people we care about without feeling worse afterwards—and without leaving them feeling bad, too—takes time, and practice.

PART TWO

A Few More Good Rules

Besides imagining how the other person is feeling and acting accordingly, here are some other things it is *always* good to do, things you can rely on to be "the right thing":

Treat people kindly, speak to them gently, thank them when they do something nice, and try to have an open heart for their apologies when they say they're sorry after they've done something unkind. Be especially kind to anyone who is younger than you are. Remember what it felt like to be younger, and how thrilled you were when someone older treated you with respect or interest.

Be as generous as you can toward people who have less than you do. Be discreet (in other words, don't brag or show off) about what *you* have.

If you see someone being hurt, do something about it. Keep in mind that it's just fine to enlist the aid of an adult—a teacher or a parent or another grown-up you know you can trust. If the situation is one you shouldn't get directly involved in (if you're in the grocery store, let's say, and you see a parent hitting a child, or you're in a playground and you see that a group of children are taunting and making fun of another child, or in any other way hurting someone, or you see someone mistreating an animal), you should get a grown-up to help *immediately*.

Below, I've listed some other basic rules for being good. Some of them are pretty obvious, and you've probably heard them all your life (for example, the first one: never take anything that doesn't belong to you) and some of them (for example, the third one, about apologizing) may be things you've never thought about before. Read them, think about them, and keep them in mind.

> Never steal anything.

> Never be cruel on purpose to anyone, even if it's someone you don't like. If you've been cruel accidentally, apologize.

> When you apologize, *mean* it. Think it through. Saying "I'm sorry" doesn't fix things; it only makes them *look* fixed. Stop and try out the golden rule in the privacy of your own mind. Ask yourself how it feels to be the other person right now. Let yourself feel and *understand* what it is you are apologizing for. *Then* say you're sorry.

> Be grateful for other people's acts of generosity and kindness. Let them know you're grateful. Never assume they'll know without your telling them. Write notes of thanks; call them up.

➢ Always treat other people with respect. This means: take them seriously, be polite, and do your best to defer to them in matters that are their own areas of expertise (if someone who is an expert ice skater tells you something about ice skating, don't say, "No, that's not the way I do it!" Even if you feel that way, keep it to yourself and at least consider the advice she's giving you. You might find that it's very helpful, even if you were annoyed when she said it). If someone voices an opinion you don't agree with—or says something that's different from what you've been told—it's okay to disagree, but do it *respectfully*. Don't be mean (never say, "That's a stupid idea," or "You're wrong!" or "I can't believe you think that!") or laugh at someone else's ideas or opinions. Just tell them what *your* ideas are. "That's interesting," you might say. "I never thought of it that way. Here's what I think..." or, "Really? You know, there are a lot of different ideas about that," and talk about what *you* think. Ask questions—real questions, not the kinds that are insults disguised as questions. (Instead of "asking" someone, "Do you *really* think that boring/terrible song [or TV show or book or movie or game] is actually *good*?", try asking her what she likes about it, or how it makes her feel.) Always remember that *everyone* deserves respect.

➤ And that includes you. Not only should you expect to be treated with respect by others—so that if someone were to say to *you*, "Are you kidding me? You *like* that dumb song? What are you, a baby?", you might respond by saying, "I do like that song. Here's why..." (and perhaps the "why" is: *because it makes me feel good...* or *because the melody is so pretty...* or *because I like to dance to it...* or *because it reminds me of this happy day I was having the first time I heard it,* or anything else that's true)—but you also should always be respectful of *yourself.* Answering a mean question in the way I've suggested is one way of respecting yourself, and that leads me to the next section of this Guide....

Take yourself seriously!

People often are subject to self-doubt and uncertainty, even "self-hate" (*I'm no good at that; I know I can't do it; nobody could possibly really like me; I'm stupid; I look foolish doing that; I'm weird; I don't fit in*—and so on.)

If you let yourself be stopped by this kind of thinking, you will miss out on MANY things that might be wonderful. If you are sure someone you're interested in being friends with won't like you, so you don't put yourself forward and talk to her or him, then there's a chance you'll never get to know that person (who might just be shy). If you're shy yourself, this may seem very difficult, so it may help to know that most people feel shy at least some of the time. Even people who seem very confident have moments (or hours or days) of self-doubt, and no one is confident in *all* situations.

Everyone would *like* to feel confident all the time—and nobody enjoys being scared—but if you can face your own anxiety (which is another way of saying "the feeling of being scared and nervous"), reminding yourself that it'll be worth it if you can make yourself speak up—or introduce yourself to someone new, or raise your hand to volunteer to do something, or audition for a play, or try some new activity you're curious about but afraid you'll be bad at—there is a very good chance that something good is just ahead.

And really, the scared part doesn't last very long. You just have to get to the other side of it! (Think of it like jumping over a big puddle. And sure—it's always possible that you'll land just short of the other side, and get your feet wet. But then one *more* little jump and you're on dry land!)

If you don't try something you're even a little bit curious about—a sport or other activity, for example—you'll miss out on the chance to do something that could be a lot of fun. And don't just try it once. *Once* may not give you enough time to find out if you like it. Try it often enough to give yourself a chance to really see if you like it or might have some aptitude at it that you don't yet know about. Sometimes it takes trying something—even something you are pretty sure (or even very sure) you're not going to be good at—to discover that you are actually very well-suited to it.

The author of this Guide didn't learn to swim until she was *thirty-five years old* because she was *sure* she couldn't do it. She was afraid to go underwater, and she was sure she'd never *not* be afraid. She also didn't try getting on a horse until she was forty-six because she was convinced that it would be too frightening. And she didn't take her first singing lesson until she was even older than that, because—well, she isn't even sure why. Maybe she just thought it would be silly, because after all she didn't expect to ever be a professional singer.

Well, she is a pretty good swimmer now, thanks to a wonderful swimming teacher who was very patient with her—and she had more fun on her two trail rides (which her daughter begged her to go on with her, because when her daughter was eight years old, she loved horses so much and wanted her mother to understand *why* she loved them) than doing almost anything else... except maybe singing, which she has learned to be pretty good at, too. She even sings in public—and although she will never be a professional singer who makes records and is on the radio or TV, being an amateur singer who practices singing every day has turned out to be a very important part of her life and makes her very happy.

You never know what's going to help you be happy until you try a bunch of different things.

So: another good general rule for living is ***Try new things!***

Then you'll know if you like them.

This goes for food, activities, books (read the first page even if you're SURE you won't like it; you never know...)—it goes for all kinds of things. ***But:***

Don't try anything that you know is dangerous or bad for you.

This is where having adults around who have experienced more of the world than you have, and who have a good idea of what is unhealthy or dangerous, is absolutely necessary. Take our word for it when we tell you something is going to do you harm.

Still, nobody can protect you from every possible danger. It's good to keep your eyes open and be aware of the possible dangers in the world around you. There will be times when only you can make the decision that will keep you safe—when you simply have to say NO, even when there's no adult around to say it for you, or advise you to say it.

If someone were to offer you a drug, for example, and tell you, "It'll make you feel great—trust me, I've taken some, and I know," it will be up to you, if you're alone with this person, to remember what you've learned and say, "Nope, not for me," and stick with that even if the other person is very insistent or teases you or makes fun of you for saying no.

Sticking to your guns—knowing what you want and don't want, and what's good for you—is one of the most important things you can do for yourself. This doesn't mean you will always feel sure about things, but it does mean that you can say NO and give yourself time to think about—or talk to an adult about— the question that was raised. The main thing to remember here is this:

Never let anyone push you into doing anything—no matter how sure they are that it's a good idea!

You are *your own person*, which means that you "own" yourself, and even when other people try to convince you that they know what's best for you—or that they know better than you do about something—you don't have to go along with it. Sometimes it's appropriate to explain yourself, and sometimes you don't have to. Sometimes it's enough just to say no. (For some tips on feeling comfortable saying no, see the next part of this Guide.)

PART THREE

Express Yourself!

This is one of the keys to a happy, "fulfilled" life. Artists know this. Even artists who aren't much for talking (like some people I won't name, who happen to be the husband of the author of this Guide, and who drew the illustrations for it) express their feelings and thoughts and ideas in their work. Sometimes these are expressed in unusual ways (for example, an artist might paint a lonely looking apple—or three brightly colored, glowing, satisfied-looking plums).

Sometimes composers of music or the people who write lyrics (the words to songs) use "hidden meaning." The Beatles might say, "She's got a ticket to ride" and really mean, "A girl I love seems like she's thinking about leaving me."

Anyway, the point is: however you do it—whether directly, in day-to-day life, by speaking about it or otherwise showing it, or indirectly, through art, it's always a good idea to EXPRESS yourself. Keeping feelings—particularly, worrisome ones—hidden inside is a good way to make yourself unhappy, or even sick.

Now, we all know there are lots of people who find they can't communicate what's on their minds. There are all kinds of different reasons for this. Sometimes it turns out that they've been *taught* that this is what they are supposed to do (and often the people who've taught them that—their parents, usually—didn't *mean* to teach them that). The writer of this Guide's own mother, for example, was taught when she was very young that it was bad to be angry. If she expressed even a tiny bit of anger, her mother would hush her, and would make her feel terrible about being angry.

The little girl's name was Sheila (it still is, although of course she isn't a little girl anymore). Sheila's mother wanted her to have only good and happy feelings, and she thought that by making sure Sheila didn't express those "bad feelings," she wouldn't feel them at all.

Well, the trouble with *that* is that not talking about feeling angry or sad or frustrated or anything else that feels bad doesn't stop the bad feelings. In fact, often this will make the bad feelings *worse* feelings. Telling someone how you feel is a relief when you're feeling bad—and expressing your anger or frustration sometimes helps you to get rid of it, or at least to help you feel a little bit better.

No one *wants* to feel bad, and who can blame Sheila's mother—or anyone—for hoping to protect her child and keep her from feeling angry? The trouble with *this* is that, as I've said, we *all* get angry, sad, frustrated, jealous, irritated, and upset. We *all* have "bad" feelings as well as good ones. And the only way to make absolutely sure you never feel anything that hurts is to stop feeling anything at all. And who would want that?

Some of us worry a lot that something terrible will happen not only if we get angry, but if we don't go along with what other people want us to do. Saying "no"—whether it's to an offer to do something dangerous, or just to an offer to do something we don't want to do because we're not in the mood or want to do something else instead—can sometimes feel as scary as letting people know that we're angry or sad or jealous. But learning to say "no" is another important part of growing up and living a safe, healthy, happy life. It takes practice—just like learning to be good at a sport or playing a musical instrument. And just like practicing the piano, or throwing a softball, or walking the balance beam—or doing the backstroke or writing a poem—the more you do it, the better you'll get at it. But just like practicing all those other kinds of activities, if you keep doing it in a way that doesn't really work (if you play the same piece of music on the piano and get the same notes wrong every time you practice it, and you never stop and just work on that one measure until you *get* those notes right—or you keep throwing the ball in a way that hurts your throwing arm, and you never try another way of doing it), you don't actually get better at it.

So you must give yourself opportunities to practice saying "no" until you get comfortable doing it. And along the way, you'll find that it gets easier, even for the shyest person.

Let's say your best friend wants you to come over to her house, and you just don't feel like it today. (Maybe you want to stay home and read, or draw. Maybe you're feeling blue and don't want to be around anyone but your mom. Maybe your mom has just proposed something for the two of you to do that sounds like fun to you. Or maybe there's another friend you've been thinking about spending time with on this day.) There are probably lots of reasons you feel uncomfortable saying no. You may be afraid your friend will get angry (and what will happen if she gets angry? Are you afraid she won't be your friend anymore?). Maybe you're worried about hurting her feelings. Maybe you think she'll think you're weird if you tell her you want to be alone—or that you were looking forward to spending the day finishing a book you're in the middle of. Maybe she'll think you're a baby if you tell her you want to spend the day with your mom. And maybe, if she knew that you wanted to spend time with someone else, she'd think that meant you didn't want to be her friend anymore—and that's not true: you just want to have more than one friend!

None of these worries you may be having are unusual or strange. Everyone has these sorts of worries. But if you decide that it's not worth the trouble to say "no" because of them—if you end up going over to your friend's house when you don't want to—you'll feel resentful, and you probably won't have any fun, and neither will she.

So even though it's hard—and sometimes it's *really* hard—you must resist the temptation to give in to your own worries (she'll think you're weird, she'll think you're silly, she'll be mad at you, she'll be hurt). One of the reasons we have friends is so that we know there are people to whom we *can* express ourselves honestly. A friend is a person you feel safe and comfortable with.

So you can say, "I love coming over to your house! Do you think I could come over tomorrow [or next Sunday, or on Thursday after school] instead? "

And go ahead and tell her what it is you mean to do with your day. If it's spending time with someone else, you can reassure her that *she's* still your best friend. Tell her why you're interested in spending time with the other girl. Maybe there's something you do with her that your best friend isn't interested in doing, or maybe this is just the first chance you've had to get to know her, and you've been curious about her. If you want to stay home and read, tell her about the book—and offer to lend it to her when you're done reading it. If you want to spend time with your mom, and you feel embarrassed about that, *tell* her you're embarrassed.

When you say "no," you don't have to leave it at *just* no.

But sometimes you can, and sometimes you should.

When someone you don't know very well wants you to do something dangerous or unhealthy, you should always feel free to say, "No, I don't want to do that." And if she or he says, "But why not? It's fun!", you should feel free to say, "I just don't" and end the conversation.

If people are angry with you, or make fun of you, for saying "no" to something that's bad for you, then these are people you will not enjoy having in your life—even if you thought you liked or admired them before. If the person urging you to do something that you know is a bad idea is someone you care about, there's no reason not to say, "And I wish you wouldn't do it either!" and even offer an alternative. If that person says, "Oh, what do *you* know?" or "What are you, a little kid?" or "So, are you scared, or what?", you may just have to say, "I only know what I think, I guess, and I think that's a terrible idea," or, "If saying no to that means I'm still 'a little kid,' I guess I am. Oh, well." Or, "Yeah. I *am* scared. And you should be, too." And then you might say, "How about if, instead of doing that, we do . . . ?"

This may seem like hard advice to take—and it *will* be hard, at first. But it gets easier. Every time you do it, it will get a little easier. And then you will have another skill you can rely on to help you in your life.

Help other people to express themselves

It may surprise you to learn that some people have just as much trouble expressing "good" feelings—the kinds of feelings that not only feel great to them, but make other people feel great too if they are expressed *to* them (love, for example)—as bad feelings. Some people can't express any feelings at all.

Perhaps you know someone who has a hard time letting others know they love them, even though it feels wonderful to love someone and would make the person who is loved feel wonderful to hear about it, or see the evidence that she is loved.

Who knows why some people can't express love or other good feelings? Maybe they've been taught that they might get hurt if they tell other people they love them, or if they show that love too much. Maybe they have the idea that letting people see that they're happy, or excited, or optimistic (that they believe that something good is going to happen, or that things will turn out well), will lead to disappointment— in other words, they think that if they express their good feelings, they will somehow *turn into* bad feelings. Maybe they imagine they'll be laughed at—or maybe they've been taught that it's not polite to get "too emotional."

Whatever the reason, the best thing you can do for someone who has trouble expressing herself is to try to create an environment (like a "small world") around her that will help her feel safe to talk about—and show—what she feels inside.

One of the best things you can do for another person is make her feel comfortable enough to express herself. This isn't always easy to do—and you yourself may feel uneasy about revealing certain things. And since it's possible that you will sometimes say things that other people won't want to hear, you need to be prepared for that outcome too, so that you can tell yourself, "Well, I knew that might happen, and it's too bad—and I wish it hadn't!—but that doesn't mean I should give up forever on saying what I feel. Maybe I can just find another way to express this particular thing to this one person. . . ."

When the author of this Guide was a child, she had a friend who would often mock her when she told her something that she meant for her to take seriously. Or—sometimes—her friend would simply change the subject: she made it clear that she just wasn't interested in talking about, or hearing about, what was on this author's mind.

But the author's friend was her favorite person in all the world! And so she just kept trying. She learned that even when her feelings were hurt, she didn't have to give up, and it was worth the effort. She and her friend ended up being good friends—best friends—for many years.

When people keep their deepest, most important feelings to themselves and don't talk them over with anyone, they start to feel terrible. Sometimes they even get stomach aches or headaches, just from keeping their feelings locked up inside them. So one of the important things to remember is that you don't have to hide your worries or other things that are making you unhappy, but you *might* have to think hard about the best way to express them or the right time to do it.

And here is one more thing you might want to keep in mind:

Everyone is the same, and everyone is also different.

Everyone gets angry sometimes, and everyone feels jealous, worried, sad, nervous...and also joyful, excited, loving—in other words, at one time or another, we all feel *everything*. We may not experience these feelings in exactly the same way, though, and we are likely to *think* about things differently, too. One of the most interesting ways to find out about the world is to ask people what's on their mind or how they feel— but it is sometimes surprising (and sometimes disappointing) to find out that the people we feel closest to may not think about things the way we do, or may not think about the same things we do—or may be thinking about the same things but not have the same feelings about them.

The fact is, everyone has private thoughts and feelings about things that shape the way they see the world. And no matter how close you are to someone else, there are bound to be differences in these private experiences. You might read the same book as your best friend and find out that you had completely different ideas about it, or that while the ending of the story made you sad, *she* didn't feel sad at all but thought the ending was funny. Or you might remember a day you spent with someone as being dull or irritating, and the person you spent it with might remember it as the most fun she'd ever had!

These differences—and all the other differences between us, from our favorite colors and the types of music we like best to our convictions (our deepest beliefs)—help to make life interesting. Express what's on your mind (your thoughts)—and in your heart (your feelings)—and let other people know how interesting *you* are. And pay attention when they let you know all the things that are interesting about them.

PART FOUR

All Play and No Work

There's an old expression that goes "All work and no play makes Jack a dull boy." Most people don't think much about the opposite, though—that "all play and no work" would also make you very "dull" (that is, boring—and *bored*). Still, it's true: if *all* you do is have fun—and you never do anything useful or help others in any way—life becomes pretty dull and begins to feel pointless.

Naturally, when you're a child you're not expected to work as hard as an adult, or to be responsible for as many things. Imagine if you had to shop for the groceries, earn the money to buy them, cook all the meals, pay the bills, repair things when they break, do the family's laundry, and so on. All of these kinds of work are things that adults do, because this work is necessary to keep things going. Someday you'll do all (or most) of them too. When people live together, in marriages and families, they share the tasks that need to be done to keep things going. But even as a child it's important to contribute to the overall well-being of the family. A chore or two—dusting, tidying up some specific area of the house or apartment, vacuuming, sweeping, helping with the cooking or cleaning up after meals—that contribute to everybody's well-being is good practice for the future, plus it makes you feel you're making a real contribution to family life, instead of just being taken care of, the way a pet is. Or a baby. Taking care of your own things—picking up your toys, clearing your dishes from the table and putting them in the sink, keeping your clothes put away and throwing the dirty ones down the laundry chute or into the hamper—are simply the daily activities required to take care of yourself, along with the things you do to take care of your body, like brushing your teeth and taking a shower or a bath.

When you were very young, other people took care of all your needs (even brushed your teeth and washed your hands and wiped your bottom for you!). Now that you are older, you wouldn't want adults to do everything for you. And if they did—if you never had to lift a finger to take care of yourself or to help the family with its regular chores—you'd begin to feel foolish and babyish.

As you get older, you'll want to take on more things for the sake of your family, as well as taking on more responsibility for yourself. You'll start doing your own laundry, and keeping track all by yourself of when school projects are due. But even now you might be ready to do some things for your family: you might want to prepare a whole meal by yourself; you might enjoy being in charge of dinner sometimes (you could use your parents as your helpers! You could read the recipe and ask them to do the parts that help prepare the food for cooking: chopping, or peeling).

And when someday you find yourself doing things that are strictly for someone else—doing someone else's laundry, say, to save them time, or packing a lunch for someone else— you'll find that it makes you feel really good. It's like giving somebody a present—which you probably already know is at least as much fun as getting a present yourself!

PART FIVE

Make New Friends but Keep the Old

What else does it take to live a healthy, happy life?

Well, life wouldn't be complete without friends.

Having people in your life whom you've *chosen* to have in it—because you've found each other and discovered that you have a natural sympathy toward each other ("sympathy" here doesn't mean "feeling sorry for" but rather "understanding"), people to whom you *feel* connected even though you're not related to them—is one of the most exciting *and* comforting things in the world.

And it is especially wonderful to have a particular or "best" friend you can count on to talk things over with, and who is interested in many of the same things you are, *and* whom you can almost always be sure of having a good time with. If you find such a person, hold on to her. While it's inevitable (or almost certain) that you will both change as time passes and you begin to grow up, the basic facts about you won't, and even if she begins to seem quite different from the girl you were close to when you were younger, she is the same person *inside*. Sometimes you may have to remind yourself that this person who is changing—who talks differently and has different ideas and interests and may even look very different—is still the girl you've known for so long and loved. And sometimes remembering this will be hard. But like so many things that are hard, it's worth doing. It's worth talking things over (and even arguing, if necessary), so that you still understand each other.

And as time passes, you'll make new friends, too. You'll have other interests and you'll meet people who share those new interests. You may end up living somewhere else and making friends who live near your new home and go to your new school—wonderful people you would never have met if you hadn't moved. The world is a big place, and it is full of people—and the more of them you meet, the more chances you have for your life to be enriched.

If you haven't made a new friend in a long time, you may feel shy or just confused about how to do that. After all, you can't very well walk up to someone who looks interesting and say, "Do you want to be my friend?" Here's a tip for making new friends—and this advice returns us to the very first piece of advice in this Guide:

Treat the other person the way you'd
like to treated.

What would make you happy to hear someone say, or to be asked?

Stop and think about that, and when you approach someone you'd like to get to know better, do so in a way that would be appealing to *you*. It's hard to go wrong when you follow that rule. It will keep you from offering empty compliments (flattery) because you know that *you* would never want to be insincerely complimented, or complimented for something that doesn't matter to you—or complimented excessively for something in a way that would embarrass you. It may help you to think about *specific* things to say, or do. It may allow you to have a moment of understanding and insight—a chance to *think about how it feels to be the other person,* even when the other person is someone you don't know very well (or hardly know at all) yet.

Paying attention to what others are interested in will give you a chance to ask questions they're likely to be happy to answer. (Don't you like it when someone asks you about something you care about or know a lot about?) Even if you feel very shy, you may be able to manage to ask a question—and asking questions is a very good way to begin to get to know someone.

It's exciting to make new friends—but holding on to the ones you already have is important, too. What the author of this Guide believes is that once you have loved someone, you love them always. Sometimes you need to remember to open up your heart again—especially after a long time passes when you haven't seen each other, and you feel a little shy in each other's presence. Then you have to go slow, and remember what brought you together before. Sometimes it helps to talk over old times, or talk about something you know you still have in common. You may even find you have a lot more in common now than you used to—that both of you have discovered a new interest in the same thing! But you may also learn about new things that will interest you too, through your old friend's interests. And you may meet and like some of *her* new friends, and expand your world in this way, too.

Friendship doesn't always go smoothly, though. Even best friends— even people who've known each other for practically their whole lives and still feel close—will sometimes argue. And it feels terrible to be in a fight with your friend, no matter what it's about. The best thing to do when you're angry with your friend is to tell her how you feel and ask her to tell you how *she* feels. If you're too angry to be able to do this— or you're ready to do it, but *she's* still too angry—then give it a little time and *then* give it a try. Even after you've talked about it, you may still be angry with each other for a while, but at least you'll both understand what you're angry about, instead of just being angry—and if you can see each other's points of view, and understand how the other feels, you'll get past the fight and back to fun. And chances are that your friendship will be stronger, too, as a result of this. Because just as it's impossible to only feel good and happy all the time, it's also impossible to get along perfectly all the time. The key to surviving these disagreements is understanding them.

Crushes, Romance, Love

This is a complicated subject, and it'll be a few years yet before you need to think much about it. But some of being a kid is preparation for being an adult, and there will certainly be feelings you'll have now that are a kind of preparation for more grown-up love, and for thinking about who you might want to spend your life with, and why.

How do people fall in love? Why do they?

Well, a lot of it is just like friendship. You meet someone who shares some of your interests or enthusiasms—or you discover this in someone you already know. But it's not just "shared interests" that make people fall in love. You probably already have discovered that there are plenty of girls who are interested in what you're interested in who nevertheless have not become your good friends. It's—again—a kind of sympathy for each other, a mutual understanding. It's how "simpatico" you are with the other person. It's how being in that person's company makes you feel. It's the kinds of things you end up talking about and the way you talk about them. It's a mixture of comfort and ease—and excitement and thrills.

When you fall in love, it's not so different from falling "in friendship." When you find a best friend, it's based in part on the thing people call "attraction" (like a magnetic pull), just like love is. But it is different, too. And that different part—the part you won't really experience till you're a little older—is one of the things that makes life sweetest.

When the author of this Guide fell in love with the man who would become her husband, it was because of a combination of things. She fell in love with the beautiful little paintings he made of fruits and candies and candles, and with his gentle manners and his kindness. She was amazed that he was able to fix anything that was broken. To her, this seemed like magic, because she'd never known anyone who could do that. That he was very shy and reserved made him an unlikely friend for her, because she was—and still is—very talkative and outgoing and sociable. Indeed, she noticed that he was so different from her, it was surprising that they could spend so much time together and enjoy it so thoroughly.

But they had what they considered to be the most important things in common: they were both devoted to the same kinds of principles—fairness and justice—and they were both very loyal people, and in some ways quite old-fashioned. They were both very serious about the work they did—the stories and books she wrote, the paintings and drawings he made—and they both were content spending a lot of time by themselves, writing or painting, reading and thinking.

The differences between them—that he liked sports and she hated sports, that she liked to garden and he had no interest in gardening, that they liked to listen to different kinds of music, that he liked the country and she liked the city better—didn't bother them very much. They felt they could trust each other, and when they spent time together they felt very comfortable. And some of the ways they were different turned out to be nice: his quietness made her feel quieter, and she liked the way that felt; her talking so much and getting so excited about things made life seem more interesting and exciting to him. And he took her to visit his family, who lived far from any city in a little house surrounded by woods, and she took him to visit hers, in one of the biggest cities in the world—and they both had fun on those visits.

But perhaps the most important thing to them both, when they thought about their future, and about what they wanted their lives to be like, was that they felt they could tell that the other would be a wonderful parent, and that if they ever had a child together, she would be a wonderful, smart and sensitive and artistic and funny and beautiful person, whom they both would love with all their hearts and take good care of, and enjoy spending time with and teaching everything they knew about life.

And this turned out to be true.

AFTERWORD

This book was written for that child, and it is dedicated to her. But it is also dedicated to you, with the author's wish that you have a wonderful, full and happy, healthy and interesting life, and the hope that this Guide is a useful starting point for you as you think about the kind of person you would like to be and what it means to *you* to be happy.

Figuring out "how to live" is not something you can do just once and be done with, like an arithmetic problem. We all make choices every day—all our lives—about how we are going to live. And it is never too soon to get started on that.

ACKNOWLEDGMENTS

The first draft of this book was written in 2001, as a gift for its author's daughter, who was then eight and a half years old.

It was written by request—ardent, insistent request—after a reading of *Little Women* and the observation (or complaint) that Marmee gave *her* daughters each a copy of a "guide to life."

"Why haven't you written a guide to life for *me*?" the daughter wanted to know. (In the case of Alcott's March girls, it should be noted, that guide was John Bunyan's *Pilgrim's Progress*, published in 1678.) I suppose it was impossible for a mother who was also a writer—or vice versa—to consider resisting, and so this Guide was born.

But until last year—when it surfaced again during a search of the daughter's bookshelves (the daughter herself having decamped to college nearly two years before) for the first volume of Maud Hart Lovelace's Betsy-Tacy series to read with a young friend—the author of this Guide had forgotten that she had ever written it. Imagine her surprise to find it! And yet there it was, neatly shelved alongside volumes of poetry and collections of plays—a homemade, rather crudely hand-stitched "book" (its author, who knows how to do a number of things, does not, unfortunately, know how to sew—but not knowing how to do something has never stopped her from trying to do it).

She sat down on the floor of her daughter's room then and there and read it through, cover to cover. How grateful and pleased she was that her daughter had kept it! And how grateful and pleased she was to learn subsequently, over long-distance conversations and emails and texts, that it had (and how and why it had) been helpful to her daughter and her friends when they were children.

The revisions for the version you hold in your hands were aided enormously by the sensible, wise questions and comments of Audrey Anne Wade, age ten, and the astute, funny (and bracing) notes provided by seven-year-old Lyra Kois, as well as the thoughtful responses of ten other seven- to eleven-year-old girls of the author's acquaintance who were kind enough to read the manuscript for her: Hazel Allison-Way, Violet Demko-Garcha, Elizabeth Foreman, Liliya Fyffe, Savita Jani, Ashton Pearson, Josephine Rosman, Fiona Sullivan, Kate Sullivan, and Lola Sophia Tanguay. The author wishes to thank them all—the Girls Editorial Panel, as she thinks of them in the aggregate—from the bottom of her heart.

And to the little girl, now all grown up, who asked her mother for a guide to life and who has over the years since taught her mother every bit as much as her mother has taught her, the author is most grateful indeed.

AUTHOR BIO

Author photo credit: © Lily Glass

Michelle Herman, the director of the creative writing program at Ohio State University, is a novelist and essayist whose most recent book, *Stories We Tell Ourselves*, was longlisted for the 2014 PEN/ Diamonstein-Spielvogel Award for the Art of the Essay. Her other books include *The Middle of Everything: Memoirs of Motherhood*, the novels *Missing* and *Dog*, the collection of novellas *A New and Glorious Life*, and *Like A Song*, a new essay collection about singing, friendship, home, and family, to be published in 2015. Born and raised in Brooklyn, New York, she has lived for many years in Columbus, Ohio, where she and her husband, the artist Glen Holland, raised their daughter Grace, who is now all grown up.